When in

...ain

...DIATE ·

...sco

...gyes

...e Library

Oxford University Press

Oxford University Press
Walton Street, Oxford OX2 6DP

Oxford New York
Athens Auckland Bangkok Bombay
Calcutta Cape Town Dar es Salaam Delhi
Florence Hong Kong Istanbul Karachi
Kuala Lumpur Madras Madrid Melbourne
Mexico City Nairobi Paris Singapore
Taipei Tokyo Toronto

and associated companies in
Berlin Ibadan

OXFORD and OXFORD ENGLISH
are trade marks of Oxford University Press

ISBN 0 19 432291 2

© Oxford University Press 1990

First published 1990
Fifth impression 1996

No unauthorized photocopying

Set by Wyvern Typesetting Ltd, Bristol

Printed in Hong Kong

Illustrations by: Alison Everitt; Jane Hughes; Hardlines;
Punch Publications—cartoons by Satoshi, Sidney Harris,
Vahan Shirvanian

Cover artwork by Joanna Graham

The publishers would like to thank the following for
their permission to reproduce photographs:

Barnabys Picture Library; Ivan J Belcher; Camera Press;
J Allan Cash; Chris Christodoulu; Colorsport; Crescent
Lodge Design Limited/Rodger Banning; Mary Evans;
Flash Photos/Dafydd Jones; Format; Sally and Richard
Greenhill; Harrison/Parrott Ltd; Hutchinson Picture
Library; International Fund for Animal Welfare; Rob
Judges; League Against Cruel Sports; National Film
Archive; Garry and Marilyn O'Brien; Rex Features; Royal
Society for the Prevention of Cruelty to Animals; West
Country Tourist Board

We wish to thank Andre Deutsch Ltd for their
permission to use 'Foreigners have souls, the English
haven't' from *How to be an Alien* by George Mikes;
Unwin Hyman for 'Little Johnny's Final Letter' by Brian
Patten from *Little Johnny's Confession*; Rita Wong for the
'gripman interview' and Edward Arnold for the
'marriage extract' taken from *Kicks 9 July 1982* and
appearing in Checkpoint 1984 (both on tape).

We would also like to thank the following for their
permission in reproducing additional artwork:

Biss Lancaster Plc; British Heart Foundation; Kentucky
Fried Chicken; Lynx; Oxfam; McDonald's; Pizza Hut;
Save the Children; Royal Society for the Protection of
Birds; and VSO.

Contents

A strange island

Did you know that in Britain:

- strangers usually don't talk to each other on trains?
- it is polite to queue for everything: buses, theatre tickets, in shops, etc.?
- people say 'thank you' when they give money to a shop assistant?
- people open presents in front of people they receive them from?
- people don't take their shoes off when they enter a house?
- people wash in their own bath water?

These are national habits. A habit is something we do very often. Sometimes these habits become customs. Our habits and customs can appear very strange to other people and it is usually foreigners who notice them.

TASK 1

- In your country do you talk to strangers?
- Do you automatically queue?
- Do you find any British habits strange and unusual?
- Do you share any of these habits with the British?

TASK 2

Imagine you are a foreigner in your own country. What would you find strange? List three of your more 'unusual' national habits.

Share your list with the class.

TASK 3

Some of our personal habits are good! Others are bad. For example, do you:

- do exercises?
- clean your teeth?
- bite your nails?
- eat in bed?
- suck your thumb?

- leave your clothes on the floor?
- do your homework?
- tidy your room?
- smoke?
- save money?

- Do you have any other good or bad habits?

TASK 4

In pairs ask your partner about his/her habits. Find out five good and five bad habits for each of you.

Example:

A *Do you get up early?*
B *No, I don't.*

You can ask the teacher for help, if you run out of ideas.

Now complete the table. Write down at least five good and five bad habits.

My partner's good habits	My partner's bad habits

Now interview other pairs in your class.

Find out how they completed their table. Are any of your good or bad habits the same?

Example:

A *Are either of you untidy?*
B *Yes, I'm untidy. What about you?*
A *I'm untidy too but C's very tidy.*

TASK 5

Everyone in the family has a routine or habit that someone doesn't like. Look at these pictures.

- Why is the girl being a nuisance?
- Why is the boy being a nuisance?

Think of the routines in your house. Make a list of them, starting with your own!

From the list choose some of the habits that your family doesn't like. Write these down in sentences.

Example:

I often leave clothes on the floor. My mother hates this.

Now write down a few things that you don't like the rest of your family doing.

Example:

Father always reads the daily paper at breakfast. I can't stand it.

Now work in pairs or groups and compare your answers.

- Are your families the same or different?

TASK 6

Work in pairs. Student A pretends to be the person in the picture. Student B asks questions like these:

- What time do you get up?
- What time do you go to bed?
- What do you do in your free time?
- Do you keep any pets?
- Do you have any good habits? What are they?
- Do you have any bad habits? What are they?

Now change roles.

TASK 7

Work in pairs. Play these roles.

Student A
You are a reporter. Interview Student B (the man or woman in the photographs below). Ask about his/her habits to complete this profile. First, team up with some of the other students playing Student A to prepare for your role.

Name	
Age	
Likes	
Dislikes	
Good habits	
Bad habits	

Student B

Choose one of the photographs above. You are the person in the photograph. Try to answer the reporter's (Student A's) questions. Team up with some of the other students playing Student B in the class and prepare for your role.

When you have finished the interview, change roles.

2

Chips with everything

TASK 1

Look at these pictures of different foods you can eat in schools in Britain.

- Which food do you think British children like best?
- Which food would children in your country like best?

Chinese food

TASK 2

Work in pairs.

Ask your partner and tick (√) the boxes in the questionnaire with your partner's answers.

a Do you like potatoes?

Yes ☐

No ☐

Indian food

b What type of potatoes do you like?

Chips ☐

Crisps ☐

Baked potato ☐

Mashed potato ☐

Others ☐

Chips

c How do you like your chips?

Thick ☐

Thin ☐

With salt ☐

With ketchup ☐

Plain ☐

Pizza

TASK 3

Make a questionnaire about something you eat in your country.

Example:

		1	2	3	4	. . .
1 Do you like rice?	Yes	✓	☐	✓	☐	
	No	☐	✓	☐	☐	
2 When do you usually eat rice?						
	at breakfast	☐	☐	☐	☐	
	at lunch	✓	☐	☐	☐	
	at dinner	✓	☐	✓	☐	

3 . . .

Find out:
- whether they like the food.
- when they eat it.
- how much they normally eat.
- how they eat the food (alone?, with meat?, with vegetables?, etc.).

Use your questionnaire and carry out a class survey. Make a graph like this:

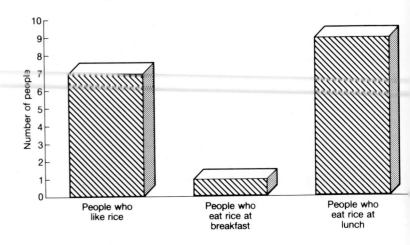

TASK 4

Foreigners often laugh at the British. They say 'In Britain you get chips with everything!' But even the British don't eat chips with their breakfast.

However, the traditional English breakfast is a big meal. Visitors to Britain often think that breakfast is the best meal of the day. These pictures show a traditional English breakfast served in many British hotels and bed and breakfast places.

As you can see it is so big that you can easily go without lunch. However, there is a lot of fat in this kind of breakfast and today many people eat a healthier one.

It is healthier because muesli and fruit juice contain less fat and more fibre. Fibre is present in plants. You don't digest it but it is useful because it helps food to go faster through your body.

Work in groups of three or four. Discuss these questions.

- What do you eat for breakfast?
  Make a list.
  Discuss which food item is healthy or unhealthy. Why?

- Would you prefer an English breakfast? Why? Why not?

- Do you eat breakfast? Why? Why not?

- Do you eat rolls or slices of bread for breakfast?

  Yes ☐   No ☐

  Do you make toast?

  Yes ☐   No ☐

  Do you put butter on your bread or toast?

  Yes ☐   No ☐

The average British family of four eats about 500g of butter each week.

- Do you eat more or less?

- Do you think butter is healthy? Why? Why not?

TASK 5

This diagram shows how food consumption in British homes is changing.

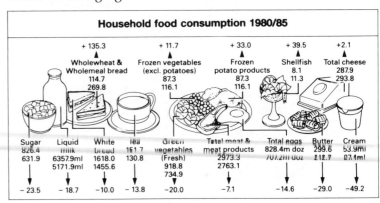

Make sentences which describe the changes.

Example:

People are drinking less tea.
People are eating less white bread.

- Have there been any changes in the way people eat in your country?
- How would you describe them?

3

Housing

a country cottage

a country mansion

a block of flats

a semi-detached house

a detached house

In Britain families like to live in houses rather than in flats or apartments ('apartments' is American English).

78% of people live in houses and only 21% live in flats.

Most houses are made of brick.

Many live in two storey terraced or semi-detached houses. Sometimes when people get older they move to a bungalow which is a house with only one storey.

A country cottage which is made of stone or a mansion is only a dream for most people.

TASK 1

Work in pairs. Look at the pictures.

- How is housing in your country different from the housing in the pictures?

Use these expressions to help you describe housing in your country:

> We've got lots of (flats, houses, etc.)
> We haven't got many (flats, houses, etc.)
> Most houses are (detached, semi-detached, etc.)
> Most houses have got (one storey, two storeys, etc.)
> Most houses are made of (brick, stone, wood, etc.)

TASK 2

Write a short description of housing in your country.

TASK 3

Hi! My name's Andy.

I live with my mother and father, my sister, Sally and our dog Minty in a semi in Cambridge. This is a plan of the house I live in! Our house has got two rooms downstairs and three bedrooms upstairs. I'm lucky. I have my own bedroom.

How about you?

A plan of a semi-detached house

Downstairs: Dining room, Kitchen, Lounge, Hall

Upstairs: Bedroom 1, Bathroom, Bedroom 3, Bedroom 2

Work in pairs or groups of three or four and ask and answer the questions.

- Do you live in a house or a flat?
- How many rooms are there?
- Have you got your own room or not? Where is it?
- Is Andy's house bigger or smaller than the one you live in?

Use these expressions to help you:

I live in a . . .
There are . . . rooms.
I've got/haven't got my own room.
My room is big/small.
There are posters/pictures of . . . on the walls.
There's a . . . in the room, etc.

TASK 4

Draw a plan of your house or flat and write a description which is like Andy's.

TASK 5

Listen to the song. In pairs write down the missing words.

Little boxes on the _____

Little boxes _____ _____ ticky tacky,

Little boxes, little boxes,

Little boxes _____ _____ _____ .

There's a _____ one and a _____ one,

And a _____ one and a _____ one.

And they're all _____ _____ _____ ticky tacky.

And they all look _____ _____ _____ .

Answer the questions:

■ What does 'little boxes' mean?
■ Translate 'ticky tacky'.
■ Are most houses just the same in your country?

11

TASK 6

Are these good or bad points for a home? Tick (√) the appropriate box.

	Good	Bad
In the town	☐	☐
In the country	☐	☐
Near a football ground	☐	☐
Near the sea	☐	☐
Near the shops	☐	☐
High up above a town or city	☐	☐
Small	☐	☐
Lots of space	☐	☐
Rooms for everyone	☐	☐
Light	☐	☐
Dark	☐	☐
Sunny	☐	☐
Damp	☐	☐
Warm and cosy	☐	☐
Quiet	☐	☐

In pairs, discuss your points. Have you ticked the same things? Do you agree? Say why you think these points are good or bad.

Draw and/or describe your ideal home to your partner.

TASK 7

houseboat

teepee

lighthouse

bender

caravan

Some people in Britain live in unusual homes. These
include old churches, windmills and some of the structures
in the photograph. Which of these unusual homes is a
'good' home. Why? Why not? Make a list of the good
points and bad points for each home.

- What other unusual homes can you think of?
- Do people live in unusual homes in your country?
- Is it better to live in a 'little box'?

13

What is a gripman?

TASK 1

Study this short history of the London tramway.

The first horse tramway opened in 1870. A ticket cost one penny.

The first electric trams appeared about thirty years later, in 1901.

The number of routes grew, but in 1952 London said goodbye to its last tram.

Today London has an underground and a bus service but no trams.

Work in pairs and try to answer these questions.

- Did you have any trams in your country in the past?
- Do you have any trams today?
- When were they introduced?
- When did they stop running?
- What are the main forms of public transport in your country today?
- Which of them do you use most often? Why?

Discuss your answers in groups of three or four.

TASK 2

Nearly everywhere in Britain trams stopped running in the 1950s, but today some British cities want to bring them back. Why do you think this is so?

Compare trams to other means of transport. Which of these statements are true (at least to some extent) and which are false? Put a tick (√) in one of the boxes for each statement.

	True	False
are faster in peak hours	☐	☐
are less expensive to construct	☐	☐
can take more passengers	☐	☐
are more pleasant to look at	☐	☐
are more fun to travel in	☐	☐
cause less air pollution	☐	☐
cause fewer accidents	☐	☐
are more comfortable	☐	☐
are cheaper to run	☐	☐
are less noisy	☐	☐

Trams . . . than buses, cars or the underground.

Trams have disadvantages as well. What are they? In pairs, write down the ones you can think of.

TASK 3

Get into two teams. In Team A there are the 'tram fans' and in Team B there are those who prefer other forms of public transport.

Argue for or against trams. End the debate by deciding whether to reintroduce trams in British towns or not. Alternatively, if there are trams in your country you could decide whether to stop them and use other forms of transport instead.

TASK 4

Now read this description from a guidebook to San Francisco.

In San Francisco cable cars are a great attraction! *Hallidie's Folly*, named after inventor Andrew Hallidie, made its first run in 1873. Today, these old-fashioned vehicles still move slowly up and down the steep hills of San Francisco. At the terminal they have to be turned back by manpower and passengers automatically lend a hand to the driver and the conductor.

The cable car can only travel along a single track on the street. It does not have a motor, but is connected to a moving cable, running under the street. The cable is turned by an electric motor in a powerhouse.

From time to time authorities have thought about stopping the cable car. In 1979, however, the citizens of San Francisco decided to launch a campaign called *Save the Cable Car!* It turned out to be so successful that the city council had to renovate the whole system, without changing its historic charm. The fleet returned in 1984!

- Do you agree with the aims of the 1979 campaign? Why? Why not?
- Can you mention any similar movement in which ordinary people had their way over the authorities?
- Has anything like this happened in your country?
- What other unusual forms of transport can you think of? Where are they? Are they historical or modern?

TASK 5

🔲 An important person in the cable car is the gripman. Listen to this interview, in which Art Luna, a San Francisco gripman for fourteen years, speaks about his job.

Suppose you spent your holiday in San Francisco.
- Would you like to work as a gripman for a few weeks? Why? Why not?
- Which part of the job would you dislike?
- Do you think a woman could be a 'gripman'?

In a group of three or four, discuss where you could take a visitor on holiday in your country for an interesting ride.

TASK 6

Look at this certificate. If you are in trouble with words, ask your teacher for help.

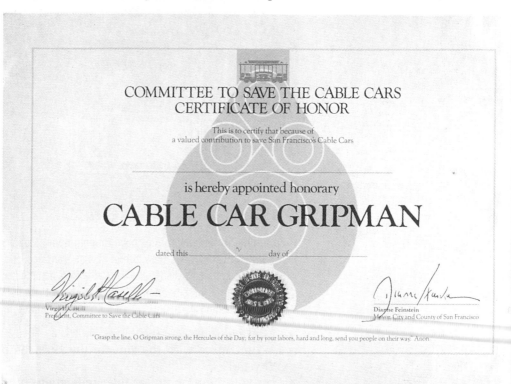

COMMITTEE TO SAVE THE CABLE CARS
CERTIFICATE OF HONOR

This is to certify that because of
a valued contribution to save San Francisco's Cable Cars

is hereby appointed honorary

CABLE CAR GRIPMAN

dated this _____ day of _____

Virgil Caselli
President, Committee to Save the Cable Cars

Dianne Feinstein
Mayor, City and County of San Francisco

"Grasp the line, O Gripman strong, the Hercules of the Day; for by your labors, hard and long, send you people on their way." Anon

- Anyone can buy this certificate for $1 in the San Francisco cable car museum. Should we take it seriously or is it just a joke?
- Do you like the short poem at the bottom of the certificate? If you do, try to translate it into your own language.

5

When in Rome 1: Manners

When we are using behaviour and ways of speaking that are good and polite we say we are using 'good manners'.

Here is an example of good manners in Britain.

A gentleman walks on the outside of the pavement when he is with a woman. Men have walked on the outside of the pavement since the time when the woman needed protection from the splashing mud of passing carts, and rubbish being thrown out of upstairs windows which usually landed on the edge of the pavement. But times change. There is greater equality between the sexes and today few men automatically walk on the outside.

TASK 1

Discuss in pairs.

In your country do men . . .

- walk on the outside?
- open doors for women?
- give women their seats in public places?

TASK 2

List some examples of good and bad manners in your country.

Good manners	Bad manners
1 _____	1 _____
2 _____	2 _____
3 _____	3 _____

Now get into groups of three or four and discuss the following questions:

- Did you choose the same examples?
- What do you mean by good manners?

TASK 3

When in Rome do as the Romans do.

- What does this proverb mean?
- Do you have a similar proverb in your own language?
- Do you think the proverb is good advice?

TASK 4

Table manners are an important part of any culture. Look at this picture of people who are eating. Each person is breaking a rule of table manners in Britain. What are they doing wrong?

Complete this advice for visitors to Britain:

When you're at the table in Britain:

- don't speak _____.
- don't reach across _____ . Ask someone to pass it.
- don't put _____.
- don't wave your _____ in the air.
- don't lift your bowl _____.

    Did you know that in Britain:

- people usually put the table napkin on their knees?
- it is polite to press your peas on to the back of your fork?
- it is impolite to make a noise when you are drinking soup?

Prepare similar advice for someone visiting your country.

20

TASK 5

At a dinner party with four or five courses it is not always easy to know which knife and fork to use. This task will help you.

List the order that the British eat these courses in.

1 The soup   **4** The meat
2 The dessert   **5** The cheese
3 The fish

Example: *Soup is the first course.*

As a general rule, start with the knife, fork or spoon that is on the outside.

Match the course to the knife, fork or spoon.

Example: *'a' is the soup spoon.*

Discuss in groups of 3 or 4:

- Do you follow the same rules in your country?
- When do you use a knife?
- When do you use a fork?
- When do you use a spoon?
- Are there other table rules in your country which are not mentioned here?

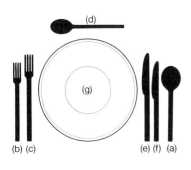

TASK 6

This is an example of a formal invitation to dinner.

- What do the letters R.S.V.P mean?
- What time should Mr and Mrs Brown arrive?

Remember:

- it is polite to reply to invitations (formal and informal).
- it is impolite to arrive late for dinner parties.
- it is polite to take a small present when you are invited to dinner. (People usually take a bottle of wine, a bunch of flowers, or a small box of chocolates.)
- it is polite to write 'thank you' notes after an invitation.

In groups of three or four reply to the invitation. First, write a reply to say you can go to the dinner. Then role-play a telephone conversation to say that you can't. (Explain why you can't go.)

Here are some expressions to help you:

. . . accept with thanks . . .	I'm afraid . . .
. . . kind invitation . . .	. . . we won't be able to . . .
I'm sorry . . .	

> Mr & Mrs Alan Smith
> request the pleasure of
> Mary and John Brown's
> company at Dinner
> on Friday, 6th January,
> at 8 o'clock
>
>   RSVP
> 7, Brookside,   01-2422
> London WC2   3128

6

When in Rome 2: Customs

TASK 1

People's nationality can also be recognized by the way they greet each other.

Look at these pictures. Match them to the descriptions below.

1 _____ 2 _____ 3 _____ 4 _____ 5 _____

6 _____ 7 _____ 8 _____ 9 _____ 10 _____

shaking hands, waving, nodding, curtsying, hugging, taking a hat off, kissing on the cheek(s), saluting, clicking the heels, bowing

■ Can you add any more to this list?

TASK 2

How often do the British use the forms of greeting listed in *Task 1*?

> **Words to help you:**
> sometimes   rarely   might   never   only

Now compare British customs to those in your country. Using the words to describe greeting from *Task 1*, write sentences.

Example:

Hugging is more/less formal in our country than in Britain.

TASK 3

Table manners or forms of greeting are part of social etiquette. However, there are other customs which run deeper. For instance, British people are said to be good listeners. In other words, it is not considered polite to interrupt the person who is just speaking. Do you?

Understatement is another character trait of the British. It is a very complex concept. George Mikes, a Hungarian by birth, knows a lot about it. Read this funny passage, which he wrote more than forty years ago.

> **Foreigners have souls; the English haven't.**
>
> On the Continent if you find any amount of people who sigh deeply for no conspicuous reason, yearn, suffer and look in the air extremely sadly. This is soul.
>
> The English have no soul; they have the understatement instead.
>
> If a continental youth wants to declare his love to a girl, he kneels down, tells her that she is the sweetest, the most charming and ravishing person in the world, that she has *something* in her, something peculiar and individual which only a few hundred thousand other women have and that he would be unable to live one more minute without her. Often, to give a little more emphasis to the statement, he shoots himself on the spot. This is a normal, week-day declaration of love in the more temperamental continental countries. In England the boy pats his adored one on the back and says softly: 'I don't object to you, you know.' If he is quite mad with passion, he may add: 'I rather fancy you, in fact.'
>
> If he wants to marry a girl, he says:
> 'I say . . . would you? . . .'
>
> If he wants to make an indecent proposal:
> 'I say . . . what about . . .'

23

- What do we mean by understatement then? In groups of three or four discuss: make up another situation to illustrate the meaning.
- Which is more characteristic of your people: understatement or overstatement?
- Are you cool and reserved as the British or rather temperamental and outgoing?

WARNING! Before you jump to conclusions, read *Chapter 15* on stereotypes.

Fast food and takeaways

TASK 1

Look at these logos of some well-known 'fast food' restaurants in the United States.

Discuss in pairs:
- Which of these fast food restaurants have you got in your country?
- Which one is the most popular?
- What is the aim of fast food restaurants?

TASK 2

Fast food restaurants like McDonald's are an American export but other countries also have fast food. For example, in the Far East, open-air food stalls serve hot food quickly and cheaply.

A Chinese takeaway

A food stall in Hong Kong

A traditional fish and chip shop
Fish and chips

In Britain however, these open-air food stalls of the orient became the Chinese takeaways, which you can find in many of the cities, towns and villages of Britain. Takeaways sell hot food you carry out to eat in another place. Takeaway food is a treat for many families. However, the most famous British takeaway is still the fish and chip shop.

What do you know about fish and chips? Work in pairs and decide if these statements are true or false. Tick (√) one of the boxes.

	True	False
1 The fish in 'Fish and Chips' is boiled.	☐	☐
2 People put vinegar on their fish and chips.	☐	☐
3 Newspaper is used to keep fish and chips warm.	☐	☐
4 The fish in 'Fish and Chips' is cut into small pieces.	☐	☐
5 People eat bread and butter with fish and chips.	☐	☐

Discuss in groups of three or four:

- What are the advantages of takeaways and fast food restaurants?
- Do you like them?
- Are there any takeaway or fast food restaurants that are typical of your country?
- What are they like?
- What do they serve?

TASK 3

Wimpy is a trademark for a fast food chain in Britain. J Wellington Wimpy was a friend of cartoon character Popeye who loved hamburgers.

Look at this menu from a Wimpy.

WIMPY MENU

Cheeseburger	£1.75	Milkshakes	90p
Hamburger	£1.50	Coca Cola	65p
King burger	£2.00	Orange juice	80p
Chicken nuggets	£1.75	Fanta	65p
French fries	60p	Coffee	60p
Icecream	85p	Hot chocolate	75p
Apple pie	85p		

In groups of three or four, discuss these questions:

- Which of the dishes can you find in fast food restaurants in your country?
- Which is the simplest? Which is the biggest?
- Which soft drinks do you like best?
- What would you choose in a Wimpy Bar?

A hot dog

TASK 4

After the hamburger, the hot dog is the great American fast food invention. As you may know, a hot dog is a sausage in a bread roll. But why is it called a hot dog?

Listen to the true story of the hot dog.

TASK 5

Listen to the tape again and decide if these statements are true or false. Give reasons for your answers.

	True	False
1 A frankfurter is a type of sausage.	☐	☐
2 Harry Stevens called a frankfurter in a roll a hot dog.	☐	☐
3 Stevens put the sausage in the roll to make it easier to eat.	☐	☐
4 The name 'hot dog' has been used since the 1920s.	☐	☐
5 Hot dogs usually taste hot and spicy today.	☐	☐

TASK 6

The hamburger is the most popular American fast food export to the world. But do you like hamburgers?

Class survey

Form groups of five students. In your group find out who dislikes or likes hamburgers and if they do, how many they eat each month. Do they eat them with mustard, ketchup or coleslaw or anything else?

On the chart, fill in the name of each student, tick (√) what they like or dislike and the name of anything else they eat with their hamburgers.

Name of student	dislikes hamburgers	likes hamburgers	eats X per month	with mustard	with ketchup	with coleslaw	with ?

Prepare a report for the class. The following expressions may help:

> The following students in our group like . . .
> They eat . . . per month
> Everybody/everyone . . .
> Most . . .
> A few of them like . . .
> No one/Nobody . . .

TASK 7

Britain's appetite for convenience foods is growing. Instead of meals many people eat crisps, snacks, nuts and cereal bars.

Many of these are made from flour or potato.

You can import one of these products into your country. Look at each product and decide which one you would import and why.

Work in small groups of three or four students.

Think about the name, the appearance, what you think it tastes like, what people in your country would like, etc.

Give your reasons to the class.

8

Ha-ha-ha!

TASK 1

⊡ Listen to this!

Did the laughter make you laugh? Why? Why not?

'The most wasteful day is that in which we have not laughed.' *Sebastien Chamfort*.

- Do you agree with this quote?
- Do you often have days when you don't laugh?
- What kind of things make you laugh?

TASK 2

'Men have been wise in very different modes; but they have always laughed in the same way.' – *Dr Samuel Johnson*

- Do you think this is true or false?

Look at these faces. Are they similar or different?

In any case, the way we laugh differs a lot from person to person. Hearty laughter is not the same as polite laughter, for instance.

⊡ Listen to these four people laughing.

Listen again, then discuss in groups of three or four:

- the age and sex of each person.
- if any of them sound like someone you know. Who?
- which adjectives suit the four laughs best:
  loud, soft, rude, hearty, unnatural, polite, scary, silly, ironical, hysterical, restrained.

1 _____

2 _____

3 _____

4 _____

- Which of them describes your partners' laughs best?

TASK 3

Look at this woman. Guess why she is laughing.

Linda Lutz is laughing because she's just discovered she's the winner of the Laughing Contest, an annual competition in San Diego, California. Linda won two prizes simultaneously. One for the longest continuous laugh (she has been laughing for four hours and one minute) and the other for the most hilarious laugh. For her stunt, she received gag prizes and a free pass to the San Diego Zoo.

In your experience, what makes people laugh in a hilarious way? List two or three things and compare them with a partner's list.

TASK 4

The scenes that made the people in *Task 2* laugh were from slapstick comedy films.

- Which of these would make you laugh?
- Can you think of other gags you have found especially funny?

In old movies *gagmen* were employed. Their job was to write jokes and funny lines for the script. Would you make a good gagman? Here is your chance to try!

The story so far . . . Three gangsters are chasing a boy. They want to catch him because he saw them rob an old millionaire in his house. The boy is running down a narrow lane when he notices that one of the thugs is waiting for him at the end of the lane . . .

In groups of four, write the script of the next take. Save the boy's life and make the gangsters look plain stupid. Each group then reads out their version to the whole class.

TASK 5

Do you read cartoon magazines, like *Punch* in Britain? Here are four cartoons from *Punch*.

Answer these questions:

- Which cartoon do you like best?
- Which one/s do you think are typically British?
- Which one could appear in your national cartoon magazines?
- What is the title of your best national cartoon magazine?
- In your view, are there national variations in humour?

TASK 6

Everybody likes jokes, but few people are good at telling jokes. We believe that it is more important *how* you tell a joke than *what* the joke is. Do you agree?

Now listen to this joke.

- Did you find the joke funny? Why?/Why not?

Organize a joke competition in the class! Choose one of your favourite jokes. Get ready to tell it to the class. As you hear the jokes, give each 1 to 5 points. Whose joke was the funniest? Who told his or her joke in the funniest way?

9

Music

bagpipes

harp

accordion

fiddle

guitar

whistle

TASK 1

Ask and answer in pairs.

- What kind of music do you prefer, classical, folk or pop?
- Do you ever go to concerts?
- When did you last go to a concert? Who was performing? What did you hear?
- Do you play an instrument, or not? Which one?
- Which of these instruments would you like to play?

TASK 2

Now listen to six extracts of folk music from the British Isles. You will hear some of the instruments in *Task 1*. Decide which part of the British Isles each extract comes from.

Extract	Comes from
1	
2	
3	
4	
5	
6	

Compare your answers in a small group and try to come to some agreement. Check your answers in the key.

SCOTLAND

Scottish piper

IRELAND

Irish dancer

WALES

Welsh harp

ENGLAND

Morris dancing

TASK 3

The following adjectives are often used to describe music. Make sure you know the meaning of each one. Use a dictionary or ask your teacher to help you if necessary.

loud	exciting	soothing	soft
strange	harsh	noisy	rhythmic
melodious	gentle	sad	
traditional	joyful	classical	

Now listen to the five extracts of music from *Task 2* again, and decide which adjectives you would use to describe each one.

Extract	Description
1	
2	
3	
4	
5	

Now work in groups of three or four and decide:

- which extract you liked best and why.
- which extracts are closest to the folk music of your country.

TASK 4

Since the 1960s, British pop music has been exported all over the world. Although most young people like pop music, there are also younger fans of classical music and every summer they go to the annual 'Proms' or Promenade concerts organized by the BBC at the Albert Hall, in London. The concerts were started in 1895 by Sir Henry Wood in a building which was destroyed in 1941. They were called 'promenades' because the audience 'promenaded' or walked about during the performance. Today, the younger music-lovers stand in front of the orchestra and fill the Albert Hall for the Last Night of the Proms.

Work in groups of three or four.

Aled Jones

King's College Chapel

A Welsh male voice choir

Look at this photograph of the *Last Night of the Proms*.
- How would you describe the audience?
- Do you have similar musical events in your country, or not?

Choose a musical event in your country and write a short paragraph describing it. Include:

- the name of the event.
- when and where it occurs.
- something about its history (who started it, when, etc.).
- an idea of who goes to it today.
- any other interesting information.

TASK 5

Aled Jones was a choir boy in the 1980s. One year he became choir boy of the year. Immediately after, he became a recording star. Then his voice changed and Aled is waiting to see what happens to his voice before he sings in public again.

Many young people sing in church choirs before their voice changes. The choir at King's College Chapel, Cambridge, which includes young boys as well as male and female adults, is world famous. A lot of males give up singing in their teens except in Wales, where there are male chapel choirs and miners' choirs in almost every town and village.

34

In a group of four ask each other:

	Student 1	Student 2	Student 3	Student 4
1 What sort of singer are you? Write *Good* or *Bad*!				
2 Do you sing in a choir?				
3 If the answer to (2) is no, where do you sing?				
4 Were you a good singer when you were younger?				
5 Where did you sing?				
6 When did you sing?				

With the rest of the class use the answers to make a survey like this:

	Number of people						
	1	2	3	4	5	6	7
Good singer now	x	x	x				
Bad singers	x	x	x	x			
Sing in a choir	x						
Sing in a pop group	x	x					

TASK 6

Young people in Britain and America like to listen to music everywhere they go, but loud music is a new health problem.

A decibel (dB) is a unit which measures how loud a sound is. Here are the decibel counts for some everyday activities.

Sound	Decibel level (dB)
Whispering	30
Normal conversation	60
Busy street	70
Noisy factory	90
Jet plane overhead	100
Thunder	110
Pop concert (near speakers)	120

A sound level of 120 dB causes pain.

Doctors have found that eight hours of listening to noises above 90 decibels results in a temporary loss of hearing and only two hours spent in 100 decibel noise causes permanent damage.

The 'walkman' is especially dangerous. Recently an ear-specialist checked forty passengers on the New York subway. They were all wearing a walkman. He found the sound volume was between 95–120 decibels!!

Work in groups of 3 or 4. Ask and answer:

- Do you have a walkman?
- If you have one, when do you listen to it?
- when you want to relax
- while you study
- in bed, before going to sleep
- while you travel or walk to school
- while you jog
- at other times

- Do you choose to:

- sit or stand near the loudspeakers?
- stay away from them?
- Why?

- What advice would you give children, your own or someone else's, on using walkmans and listening to loud music? You might find these expressions useful:

Why don't you . . .
I think/I don't think you should . . .
If I were you, I would/wouldn't

10

A question of sport

TASK 1

Work in pairs.

- What are these sports called in English?
- Which of these sports are popular in your country?
- Which of these sports do you enjoy watching?
- Which of these sports do you do, if any?
- Which of these sports would you like to do?

a

b

c

d

- Can you name these American sports?
- One of these sports is the fastest growing team game in Britain. Which one?
- Are any American games played in your country? Which one(s)?

Compare your answers with the class.

TASK 2

Read this text.

A country walk

Less than half the population of Britain take part regularly in sport. The majority of those who do are men between the age of 20 and 45. The most popular outdoor sporting activity is walking (two miles or more).

The most popular indoor activity is snooker and the similar games of billiards and pool.

This table shows the top eight indoor and outdoor sports, games and physical activities that adults in Britain take part in.

A yoga class

Outdoor		Indoor	
Walking	18.6%	Snooker/billiards/pool	8.0%
Swimming	3.7%	Swimming	7.2%
Football	2.7%	Darts	6.9%
Golf	2.2%	Keep fit/yoga	3.0%
Athletics (incl. jogging)	2.0%	Squash	2.5%
Fishing	2.0%	Badminton	2.2%
Cycling	1.8%	Table Tennis	1.4%
Tennis	1.1%	Bowls/ten pin	1.1%

- Were there any surprises?
- What would the same list in your country include?

TASK 3

> Competitive sport and the discipline of team games have always been an important part of school life in Britain. They were seen as a way of encouraging team spirit. Today, however, there has been a change of emphasis in many schools away from the traditional team games such as football, rugby and cricket, to individual sports like track and field, gymnastics or swimming.
>
> Some teachers argue that team games are elitist because only the best take part while the majority of the students can only watch. It is better to have 'sport for all', they claim, encouraging all students to take part, regardless of their ability. The emphasis should be on individual sports, which teenagers can carry on into adult life.

In groups of three or four discuss the statements below. Decide which statements you agree with. Re-write any you disagree with.

Some educationalists in Britain feel that:

- taking part in sports helps to develop the character of young people. That is why all young people must take part in sport.
- team games develop team spirit and working together.
- team games encourage people to be competitive.
- children should not play team games in school.
- 'fair play' and 'playing the game' is more important than winning.
- individual sports develop the individual more than team games.

Now discuss these questions:

- What games did your parents play in school?
- Do you play the same games today?
- List three sports that:
- your sports teacher encourages you to do.
- you like doing best.

TASK 4

Football fans sometimes damage trains and property near football grounds, attack supporters of other teams and fight on the terraces of the football stadiums.

In Britain they are known as 'football hooligans'.

In Europe, football hooliganism is known as the English disease, although there are hooligans in other countries too!

Some psychologists feel that these people enjoy fighting and they are attracted to football because the game has a 'macho' image. Others blame social problems like unemployment and alcohol as well as a lack of discipline in schools. Some people also feel that attention from the newspapers and television encourages violence.

Work in pairs and discuss these questions.

- What do you think a 'macho' image is? Give examples.
- What do you think causes football hooliganism?
- What other forms of hooliganism are there? Do they have the same cause?

Get together with another pair to form a small group and decide on ways in which you can prevent hooliganism in society.

TASK 5

Work in groups of three or four.

Read the text and discuss the questions. Be ready to report your conclusions to the class.

In Britain, women are trying to gain equality in every area of life, including sport. Today women can take part in many sports that were only for men such as boxing and body building but some doors are still closed.

For example, the English Football Association does not allow women to compete against men. In 1975 there was an appeal against the ban and the judge in the high court supported the Football Association. He said:

'Women have many qualities superior to those of men, but they have not got the strength or the stamina to run, kick or tackle and so on . . .'

But is this really true? In a recent case a teenage girl who won a prize to attend an all-male football summer school was stopped from playing competitively with boys of her own age despite the fact that she was better than many of them.

- What do you think about girls being allowed to play football with boys?
- Do you think there are male sports and female sports? Why?/Why not?

Are you of age?

TASK 1

- What are these?
- Why is there a key?

In Britain, a twenty-first birthday party traditionally marks 'the coming of age'. Today, this tradition is less important because young people get so many rights before they are twenty-one. For example, in Britain young people have the right to vote at the age of eighteen. Now, the eighteenth birthday is becoming as important as the twenty-first.

- When does one come of age in Britain?
- When does one come of age in your country?
- Do you celebrate this in any way?
- What can you do after that birthday that you could not do before?

TASK 2

Work with a partner to complete this guide of what you can or can't do at different ages.

	Age in the UK	Age in my country
You must go to school	5	
You can drink alcohol in private	13	
You can buy a pet without your parents being there	12	
You can get a part-time job	13	
You can leave home without permission of your parents	16	
You can get married if your parents agree	16	
You can leave school and work full-time	16	
You can apply for a passport	16	
You can drive a car but not a lorry	17	
You can go to prison	17	
You can vote	18	
You can drink alcohol in public	18	

TASK 3

Make a list of things young people can't do in your country because they're too young.

Discuss your list in groups of three or four.

- What things are in more than one list?
- Do you agree that young people should not be allowed to do these things?
- Would their parents let them do the things in your list? Why? Why not?

43

A generation gap

TASK 4

In Britain, people sometimes talk of a generation gap. In extracts one and two we asked some parents the question, 'What's wrong with today's teenagers?'

Then we asked some teenagers, 'What's wrong with your parents?' Here is what they said.

Listen and write down the main points in each of these three extracts.

Discuss in groups of three or four.

- Do you agree with any of the main points you heard in the interviews?
- What do parents think of teenagers in your country?
- How do you see the older generation?
- Are they boring?
- Are they friends?
- Are they people who stop you doing what you want?
- Are they something else? What?
- How can you avoid a generation gap?

TASK 5

Here is a situation.

Susan is sixteen. Every year she, her parents and her younger brother who is fourteen go on a family holiday to their home by the lake. A week before her holiday her boyfriend Andrew who is eighteen asks her to join him and a group of friends on a camping trip. She wants to go but knows that it will not be easy to persuade her father. Also, she does not want to upset or disappoint them. She decides to speak to her father and mother after dinner.

- What would you say if you were Susan?

Work in small groups of three or four and role play the conversation between Susan and her parents.

When you have finished, discuss your role play:

- Was the conversation real?
- What areas can you improve?

Practise the role play again and then show it to the class.

12

Learning to drive

TASK 1

- Can you drive yet?
- Would you like to learn? Why? Why not?
- Do you know anyone who had trouble learning to drive? What happened? Do you think some people just can't drive?

TASK 2

In most countries learner drivers need to take a test before they are allowed to go out on the roads on their own. The system however varies from country to country.

- In Britain all learner-drivers need to display 'L' plates.
- In California, USA there is no law that says a learner driver needs to have 'L' plates or any such warning device.
- In California, USA a young person can apply for a learner's permit at the age of 15½ and take a test at 16.
- In Germany you must go to a professional driving school to learn to drive.
- In Finland you have to do a written test.
- In Spain and France new drivers carry a sticker to show that the vehicle has a maximum speed of 90 k.p.h.

Work in groups of three or four or as a class and collect together as much information about the system for learning to drive in your country as you can.

TASK 3

Compare the system for learning to drive in Britain with the one in your country.

In Britain	In my country
You can learn to drive from the age of 17.	
You need to have a provisional licence.	
You need to have 'L' plates on the front and back of the car.	
You need to have a qualified driver next to you (i.e. someone who has taken a test). You don't need to have a professional instructor.	
You take a practical exam to show you can drive safely. You don't need to take a written test but the examiner asks you a few 'safety' questions at the end.	
During the test you don't have to drive on a motorway or at night.	

TASK 4

The most important part of the Highway Code is the traffic signs. But can you recognize them? Check your knowledge!

Match the captions to the signs.

A   B   C   D

E   F   G   H

1 No entry ___	5 One-way traffic ___
2 Minimum speed limit ___	6 Double bend ___
3 Parking place ___	7 Route for cyclists ___
4 Slippery road ___	8 Give way ___

■ In your home country, do you have the above signs?
■ Do you have some other signs which are specific to your country?

Now work in pairs. Student A draws a traffic sign, Student B tries to name it. Then it is Student B's turn to draw a sign. Keep changing roles.

TASK 5

At the end of the test, a British driving examiner asks a candidate a few questions. Here are some typical ones.

- What should you check in your car before going on a long journey?
- When should you switch your headlights on?
- What would you do if one of your tyres burst when you were travelling at speed?

In pairs, discuss how you would answer these questions. Think of three similar questions to ask the other students in the class.

TASK 6

Work in pairs. Imagine you are a driving instructor. Use the diagram to help you work out a set of instructions on how to start a car and move off safely.

Compare what your instructions are with this taped extract from a driving lesson.

13

Cruelty to animals?

The Island of Moreau is a novel by H G Wells. The story is set in 1887. The storyteller visits an island of 'beast men'. They were animals once but now they can talk. They are the results of experiments by Dr Moreau, who created them for fun. The animals suffer a lot because they are neither man nor beast. Before long, the monsters change back into animals. They take revenge on Moreau.

The storyteller escapes and returns to civilization but he is no longer happy because he sees people he meets as other beast people.

The Island of Dr Moreau is fiction but are we any better?

TASK 1

Work in pairs or in groups of three or four.

Here are some pictures showing how we treat animals . . .

- Do any of the pictures show cruelty to animals. Why?
- Say why the other pictures do not show cruelty.

List any other ways we are cruel to animals.

- Which ones would you stop now?

ANIMALS
The British and their treatment and attitudes to animals

There are six and a half million dogs and six to eight million cats in Britain. This means that approximately one in ten people own a dog or cat. Every year the British spend over 1½ billion pounds on pet food such as tinned dog food. They also support over 380 charities and societies which aim to protect animals. These include donkey sanctuaries, horses' rest homes, and dog and cat sanctuaries. The RSPCA (The Royal Society for the Prevention of Cruelty to Animals) is the largest animal welfare society in Britain. It provides practical help to animals in homes, hospitals and clinics. However, it also campaigns against animal cruelty. It has over 250 inspectors who make sure nobody breaks the laws which protect animals.

Each year, the RSPCA receives more money than the NSPCC (The National Society for the Prevention of Cruelty to Children).

The Bransby Home of Rest for Horses looks after about 100 rescued horses, ponies and donkeys.

The International Fund for Animal Welfare (IFAW) campaigns to stop cruelty in different parts of the world.

The Animal Liberation Front works for empty cages, not better cages. It is ready to use violence and sometimes attacks people and places which do experiments on animals.

Lynx works against the fur trade.

However, there are still 250,000 homeless dogs in Britain. People still go fox hunting and the sport of dog fighting is coming back.

It takes up to 40 dumb animals to make a fur coat.

But only one to wear it.

If you don't want millions of animals tortured and killed in leg-hold traps, don't buy a fur coat.

LYNX
Fighting the fur trade
PO Box 509 Dunmow, Essex Tel: 0371 2016

TASK 2

Discuss these questions in groups of three or four.

- Do any of you have a dog or cat?
- Do you feed it any special food?
- Do you think the British are a nation of animal lovers? Why? Why not?
- Do you think any of the charities or societies mentioned above are good causes?
- Would you give money to any of these groups?
- If you could help one group, which one would you help?
- Are there similar societies in your country? Are any of them British?
- What do you think of 'sports' like fox hunting and dog fighting?
- Are there any similar sports in your country? Do you think these sports should be banned?

TASK 3

Work in groups of three or four.

This is a poster from a forest in California.

- What is the purpose of the poster?
- Why are the actions 'careless, thoughtless and dangerous'?

WANTED!
Fred and Winifred Visitor

- Seen leaving food unattended
- Seen 'baiting' a bear with peanut butter for cute photo
- Seen leaving garbage at picnic areas
- Seen leaving food overnight in their car

These careless, thoughtless and dangerous actions are
RESPONSIBLE FOR THE KILLING OF A BEAR
PLEASE
- store your food properly
- put garbage in the trash cans
- enjoy all wildlife from a distance

51

TASK 4

There are many arguments for and against vivisection. The table below contains some of them but would *you* stop vivisection if you could?

Discuss each of the arguments carefully. Think of any new arguments you can and come to a conclusion acceptable to everyone in your group.

For	Against
Animal tests are essential. Without them drugs like insulin would not be developed.	Animals are not only used for medical reasons, but also for cosmetics.
Future tests are needed to cure cancer, for example.	Animals are used for chemical warfare tests.
Cosmetic tests make sure beauty products don't cause skin problems or cancer.	Failure of drugs like thalidomide show animals are not a good guide to human reaction.
The use of animals can help us understand the effects of smoking.	Man does not need to smoke so the cruelty to animals is unjustified.
The animals used are mainly specially bred rats and mice.	The experiments are very cruel and any use of animals is wrong.
We use anaesthetic and the animals cannot feel the pain.	Many of the animals are killed after the experiments.
It is easy to make any surgery or experiment sound cruel.	Animals cannot defend themselves or object to surgery. We must protect them.

TASK 5

Vivisection is only one of the problems affecting animals as this extract from an advertisement for the World Wildlife Fund for Conservation (now the Worldwide Fund for Conservation) shows.

The Giant Panda needs your help to survive

ONCE every eighty to a hundred years the bamboo forests in China's Sichuan Province burst into flower and then die off. And that's bad news for the Giant Panda, which depends for its survival on huge amounts of bamboo.

But that's just one of the problems facing the Panda.

To ensure that it has a future it is vital to preserve the complex eco–system in which it lives, to carry out research into its dietary needs and investigate possible alternatives, to discover the reasons for its low reproduction rate, to study the problem of internal parasites – all these factors and many more which threaten its survival.

Destruction of the environment, killing of animals for their skins or food, etc. are just some of the problems that animals face. The number of animals that risk becoming extinct is increasing every day.

Individually or in pairs:

- choose any animal which is at risk.
- collect as much information about it as you can (photographs etc.).
- find out the reasons why the animal is at risk.
- find out the action we need to take to help the animal survive.
- present your information in the form of a short five minute talk or a poster display.

Decide as a class on a way in which you can help a conservation group.

53

14

The charity industry

A charity is an organization that raises money for a particular purpose such as helping the old.

In 1988 there were 157,000 registered charities in Britain and the money collected by these charities was worth £12.6 billion.

There are charities for every area of life and people give and collect money in many different ways.

Logos of some well-known UK charities

TASK 1

Work in pairs.

Look at the logos of the UK charities.

- What areas do you think they work in?
- Do you have similar organizations in your country? Are they charities?
- Do you have many charities in your country?
- When was the last time you gave money to a charity?
- What was the charity? Why did you give to that charity?
- Now discuss the meaning of this saying:
  Charity begins at home, but should not end there.

Compare your answers with another pair.

TASK 2

Stay in your groups and read this text.

In Britain, people give help and money to charity in different ways, and for different reasons.

It is quite common for people to arrive on the doorstep of a favourite charity with a valued possession. For example, someone gave the British Heart Foundation his late father's watch.

Oxfam has received thousands of pounds from families who have sold their homes to give money to charity.

One woman saw the photographs of a starving African family in a Sunday newspaper and she sent Save the Children money for their Sunday lunch. She has been doing this ever since.

Some people give money for a special purpose. For example, The RSPCA (The Royal Society for the Prevention of Cruelty to Animals) got £1.7 million from an animal lover to help them prosecute people who were guilty of cruelty. But gifts of money for specific items can be a problem. For example, a man gave thousands of pounds so that the children who were in hospital at Christmas could get presents. As most of the children go home, a few children got some very expensive presents.

Many charities get letters from people enclosing fifty pence or a pound. There is usually a note saying, 'This is all I can give.'

The government, the armed forces or commercial firms sometimes help charities by providing helicopters and transport.

Some people leave all their money to charities when they die. Their familes often object.

The author J M Barrie gave the royalties of *Peter Pan* (the author's share of the money from the sales of the book or the selling of the story for films and theatre) to the Hospital for Sick Children in Great Ormond Street over fifty years ago. The story was, and is, very popular, so the Hospital got a lot of money from this. Now, after fifty years anyone can use the story of *Peter Pan* without payment so the hospital needs more money.

Look at each 'case'.

- Do you think it is a good way of giving? Why? Why not?
- What do you think is the best way of giving?
- How would you give money to charity?

Collecting for charity

CLEAN WATER – SO PRECIOUS FOR LIFE

An appeal for money

A sponsored tap dance

COLLECTING FOR CHARITY

In Britain, there are so many charities that they have to compete for money from the public and find different ways to collect money. In many British towns and cities, you can see people collecting money in a tin. You usually get a badge or a sticker if you put money in the tin.

Volunteers put collecting envelopes through the door of homes in their area and return to collect them.

Charities send letters and brochures asking for help. They find printed handwriting and photographs help.

People of all ages take part in sponsored events. In a sponsored event you try to get your family, friends, and even strangers, to agree to pay a sum of money if you do something. For example, you may ask people to pay money for every hour that you tap dance.

There are also big charity events and concerts, such as the Live Aid Concert on July 23, 1987 or Run for the World. These depend on television to attract help and sponsorship from all over the world.

Radio and Television also help. They broadcast appeals when there are disasters and once a year there are programmes which aim to raise money. The programmes show sponsored events and people telephone to give money to sponsor people. Sometimes they also offer money in return for 'prizes' such as a football signed by the England team, a chance to have dinner with a famous person, etc. – the prize goes to the person who offers the most money.

Live Aid

Run for the World

TASK 3

Work in groups of three or four.

- What are the advantages and disadvantages of each way of collecting money?
- Which way would work best in your country?
- How could you collect for charity? What sponsored events could you take part in?

Now do this.

You have decided to use the world of entertainment to draw attention to the problems of a group of people, e.g. the starving in Africa. Your aim is to get lots of people to help them. Which of these choices would be the most effective? Which one would be the least effective? Put the choices in order. Put 1 for the most effective, 6 for the least effective and discuss your reasons.

☐	a play about the problem which is translated into all the major languages.
☐	a specially written pop song.
☐	a world-wide television concert of classical music.
☐	a Hollywood film.
☐	a world-wide television documentary about the problem.
☐	charity concerts by people from the area.

TASK 4

Look at this advertisement for a Charity Event in the UK.

I am writing to invite your group to take part in this year's 'Breakaway'.

The rules are simple: the aim is to get people to sponsor you to travel as far away from Cambridge as possible in 24 hours. You can decide to breakaway to Czechoslovakia or just up the road to Cherry Hinton. Last year, one group made it to the Canary Islands.

There are only two rules:

1 You mustn't spend any money on transport there or back.

2 You have to enter for one of these categories:

- travelling on any form of public transport but in fancy dress

- travelling in any form of home-made transport, e.g. a 'bath on wheels'

- travelling entirely on water

- travelling on foot in fancy dress

- travelling on roller skates or skateboard all the way.

Work in small groups of three or four.

Imagine that you are going to take part.

Choose a category.

Decide what you're going to wear, how you're going to travel, etc. Present your plan to the rest of the class. Vote on the most interesting and original plan.

15

At a guess

TASK 1

Look at these photographs. What kind of jobs do these people have? Match the photos with the occupations in the list below.

1 _____

2 _____

3 _____

4 _____

5 _____

6 _____

editor, removal man, farmer, architect, university student, street cleaner

Check your answers. How many did you get right?

TASK 2

Discuss these questions in small groups:

- Describe the people above.
- Do they look different from what their occupation suggests?
- Can you describe how you imagine they *should* look?
- Why do you imagine you think in this way?

These phrases will help you:

> S/he seems/doesn't seem to be . . .
> S/he looks so . . .
> S/he doesn't look like . . . at all.
> His/Her face looks a bit/rather/quite/very . . .

TASK 3

Most people think in stereotypes. For example, for many this is a typical English gentleman.

Are most English men really like this? Stereotypes are generalizations, but usually we do not know whether they are true or false.

For example some typical stereotypes are:

- The Chinese are superstitious.
- The Italians are religious.
- The English are cold.

In pairs, add some more stereotypes to the list. In your experience, are these statements true or false?

TASK 4

Many American movies are about the fight between the *good guys* and the *bad guys*. The good guys are usually very handsome while the bad guys are ugly.

Look at the six film stars below. Can you name them?

1 _____

2 _____

3 _____

4 _____

5 _____

6 _____

Robert Redford   Humphrey Bogart   Sylvester Stallone
Henry Fonda   Paul Newman   John Travolta

In groups of three or four discuss these questions:

- Do you remember any movies starring the Hollywood actors in the photos?
- Can you think of any films where the good guys are not good-looking?
- 'American movies are written by the half-educated for the half-witted.' (*St. John Ervine*) Do you agree with this statement? Why? Why not?

TASK 5

Some people say that parts of your face and body can be characteristic of your personality. In some cultures, for example, they believe that a person with a high forehead is intelligent.

Do these have a 'meaning' in your culture?

thin lips _____

long fingers _____

blue eyes _____

pointed nose _____

Compare your answers with a partner. Do you agree? Why? Why not?

Make a list of other common stereotypes. Discuss in groups.

TASK 6

Sometimes, people dress in a certain way in order to become part of a group. For example, students in Britain often wear a college or university scarf, an anorak, and have slightly long or untidy hair.

- What does a typical student in your country look like?
- Make a list of other people who dress in a way that intentionally makes them a stereotype.

Choose one from your list, make a description of him/her. The rest of the class have to guess the stereotype you are describing.

TASK 7

In pairs, make up a short story about these people. Make your story as stereotyped as possible! Tell your story to the class. The *least* original version wins!

16

Parents and teenagers

TASK 1

[icon] Read and listen to this poem several times. Underline any words or expressions that you are not sure of and discuss them in pairs or small groups.

Little Johnny's final letter

drain – empty water from

classified – added to the list of missing young people
shreddies – a type of breakfast food
done with – finished

> Mother,
> I won't be home this evening, so
> don't worry; don't hurry to report me missing.
> Don't drain the canals to find me,
> 5 I've decided to stay alive, don't
> search the woods, I'm not hiding,
> simply gone to get myself classified.
> Don't leave my shreddies out,
> I've done with security.
> 10 Don't circulate my photograph to society
> I have disguised myself as a man
> and am giving priority to obscurity.
> It suits me fine:
> I have taken off my short trousers
> 15 and put on long ones, and
> now am going out into the city, so
> don't worry; don't hurry to report me missing.
> I've rented a room without any curtains
> and sit behind the windows growing cold,
> 20 heard your plea on the radio this morning,
> you sounded sad and strangely old.
>
> *Brian Patten*

Discuss these questions in groups of three or four.

- How old do you think Johnny is?
- Why has he written to his mother?
- Why do you think he ran away?
- Do you know anyone who has tried to leave home? What happened? Share your story with the other students.

TASK 2

In Britain today, more and more young people want to be independent and live apart from their parents. Some go in search of work or a more exciting life. Others want to escape from their homes which are overcrowded or unhappy. Some leave home with the help of their parents whilst others run away.

Listen to three young people talking about leaving home. Write brief notes of what they say.

	Extract 1 Lavinia	Extract 2 Jane	Extract 3 Zara
When she left			
Why she left			
What she does			
Where she lives			

- Which one do you think is most typical of British teenagers who leave home?

TASK 3

Read this text.

About 20% of British teenagers leave home between the ages of 16 and 20. Some are students. They get help from the government (grants) or their parents to study away from home but they go back home during their holidays so they have not really left.

Most of the 20% are like Jane. They leave home because they want to get work and experience of the world. However, accommodation is a big problem. Very few are like Lavinia. Sometimes young people share flats, but most young people have to live in bedsitters which are rooms you sleep and live in. Some bedsitters have washing and cooking facilities.

Sometimes, young people live in empty houses. This is called squatting. There are also hostels for the homeless. Apart from accommodation the main problems are loneliness, getting a job and being able to do the washing, cooking, etc. In Britain, however, it is natural for children to leave home. In fact, only 9% of people aged over 65 live with their children and many older parents who cannot look after themselves have to live in old people's homes.

A typical bedsitter

A squat

A hostel

An old people's home

Work in groups of three or four. Look at the following statements. Underline those you agree with, and re-write those you do not agree with, expressing the opinions of everyone in your group.

1 Young people should only leave home after they are married.
2 Young people should never leave home without their parent's permission.
3 Young people who live at home should pay rent to their parents.
4 Young people should only stay at home when they can't find anywhere to live.
5 Young people who leave home are selfish.
6 Young people should be allowed to go to court to 'divorce' their parents.
7 The state should help young people find a home of their own.
8 Young people should allow elderly parents to live with them.

Now discuss:

- Do young people leave home in your country? Why? Why not?
- Would you want to leave home soon? Why? Why not?
- Do you agree with this proverb?
  Home is where the heart is. (*Pliny the Elder*)
- Do you have similar proverbs in your language?
- Try to summarize the advantages and disadvantages of leaving home as a young person.

Discuss these points with the whole class if there is time.

EAT UP YOUR DINNER. THERE ARE MILLIONS OF YOUNG PEOPLE STARVING IN THE WORLD!

TASK 4

Parents and teenagers can live happily together if they try to understand each other better. But what do British and American parents mean by some of the things they say?

The most common expression British and American teenagers hear is 'No', but the ones listed below are very common as well:

1 Don't give me those excuses!
2 Let me put it another way . . .
3 I don't have time now, maybe later.
4 It's for your own good.
5 Just wait till you have kids of your own.
6 What in the world do you think you're doing?
7 Be nice to . . . , or else!
8 When I was your age . . .
9 Clean your room.
10 Are you lying to me?
11 Can't you understand what I'm trying to tell you?
12 Who do you think you are anyway?
13 Why don't you grow up?
14 Don't speak to me like that!

Work in groups of three or four.

- Translate all the sentences.
- Discuss what parents mean when they use them. Are they often heard in your language too?
- Agree on the three that you hear most often and write a short dialogue containing them.
- Read your dialogue to the class and vote to decide on the most realistic conversation.

TASK 5

Dear Abby,

This letter is addressed to all parents or adults who look after young people. I hope it will help them understand us better.
– Don't ever search your kid's room while he/she is out
– Don't read their diary or personal letters
– Do hug your kid
– Do tell them you are sorry, or that you made a mistake once in a while
etc.

Yours sincerely

(A typical teenager)

This is part of a letter a teenage girl wrote to an agony column.

Write your own letter of 'Dos and Don'ts'.

When you have finished discuss your letter with the other students in your group.

17

Marriage

TASK 1

Read this introduction and answer the questions below.

In Britain, marriage is a relationship where a man and woman make a legal agreement to live together.

The agreement can be religious (such as in church) or in a civil ceremony. Today only 50% of people get married in church. Young people under sixteen can't get married. When you are sixteen and seventeen your parents must agree. The number of teenage weddings is dropping. Only 28% of brides and 11% of bridegrooms are under 21. 32% of brides and 33% of grooms are aged 21–24.

The average age for men to get married is 25½. The average age for women is 23.

One in ten British couples get divorced in the first six years. The younger the couple, the more likely the divorce.

Discuss these questions in small groups.

A church wedding

- Do you want to get married? Why? Why not?
- When do you want to get married – between 18 and 21, between 22 and 25, between 26 and 30 or after 30?
- How old do *you have to be* to get married in your country – under 16, 16 and over, 18 and over?
- What do you think of societies where girls get married when they are 8 or 9?
- Do most people get married in a civil or a religious ceremony?
- What is the average age of brides in your country? (If you are not sure compare your answers with other students and see if you can find out.)
- What is the average age of grooms in your country?
- How common is divorce in your country?

A civil ceremony in a Registry Office

TASK 2

Read this description of the steps to marriage in a Church of England wedding.

The first step is the *engagement*. To mark this, James gives Carol an *engagement ring*.

James and Carol decide on a church wedding and arrange a date with the vicar of their local church. For three weeks *banns* are read out to tell the people that Carol and James want to get married.

On the day of the wedding James arrives first with a friend. The friend is the *best man*. James waits at the altar with the best man.

Carol arrives later with her father, her *bridesmaids* and a *page boy*. Carol follows tradition by being late and wearing white. For luck, she wears

Something old, something new,
Something borrowed and something blue.

She walks up the aisle with her father by her side. The bridesmaids and page boy help with the flowers and dress.

After Carol's father gives her away, she and James take the marriage *vows*:

'I James take thee Carol to be my lawful wedded wife, to have and to hold from this day forward, for better or worse, for richer for poorer, in sickness and in health, to love and to cherish, till death do us part, according to God's holy ordinance; and thereto I plight thee my troth.'

'I Carol take thee James to be my wedded husband, to have and to hold from this day forward, for better or worse, for richer for poorer, in sickness and in health, to love, cherish and obey, till death do us part, according to God's holy ordinance; and thereto I plight thee my troth.'

The vicar blesses the *wedding ring* and places it on the third finger of the bride's left hand. These days, the groom often wears a ring too. As they leave the church together, their friends throw *confetti* and *rice*. The friends and family go to a *reception* where there is a lot of food and drink. They drink a toast to the bride and groom, eat a slice of wedding cake and listen to the speeches. During the reception Carol changes from her wedding dress into her going away clothes and they go off for a *honeymoon* in Portugal.

Now work in a small group and discuss these questions:

- How is Carol and James's wedding similar or different from a wedding in your country?
- What do the couple promise each other in the marriage vows?
- Do you think the vows are suitable for the modern world?

TASK 3

One tradition in Britain is that friends of the bride and groom decorate the car the couple will go away in.

But as this photograph taken at a society wedding in Bombay, India, shows, there are colourful wedding traditions in other parts of the world too.

In groups of three or four aim to make an album or display that illustrates some of the wedding traditions in your country. Here are some ideas:

- Use your own sketches and drawings or photographs from magazines, newspapers or your family album and write captions for them.
- Translate sayings, vows, etc.
- Write a description like the one in *Task 2*.

Make your album as interesting and colourful as possible.

TASK 4

In Britain most people date and marry:

- people they live near.
- people they work with.
- people they go to school and university with.

A mixed marriage

Most choose to marry people they find attractive and they usually choose people of the same nationality, race, religion and educational background. They also marry someone who is roughly the same age. Because Britain is a multi-racial community mixed marriages are more common today but they are still the exception.

- Who do people marry in your country?
- Do you know anyone who married a person who:
- is a lot older?
- is from a different nationality, race or religion?
- came from a very different educational background?
- What happened? Are they happy?
- Discuss the advantages and disadvantages of marrying someone from a different background or culture.

TASK 5

In arranged marriages the parents choose the person who their son or daughter will marry. Arranged marriages are very common in India and Pakistan. In Britain, there is a large community which came from these countries and arranged marriages are still common.

- Is there a tradition of arranged marriages in your country?
- What do you think are the advantages and disadvantages?
- What are some of the problems of arranged marriages in a society like Britain?

 Aneeta is nineteen. She lives in England. She married Hitesh who is twenty-three. It was an arranged marriage. Listen to her view on arranged marriages.

- What does Aneeta think of arranged marriages?
- What does she see as the advantages?
- Do you agree with her?

An Indian marriage

Tapescript

UNIT 3 Housing

TASK 5

(song of 'Little Boxes')

UNIT 4 What is a gripman?

TASK 5

Question What does a cable car gripman do?

Al Well, he drives the cable car, so to speak. He does not have to steer of course, but he grips the cable using levers. To stop, he releases the grip on the cable and steps on the brakes.

Question How fast can the cable car travel?

Al Nine-and-a-half miles an hour.

Question Is this an easy job?

Al Come on, man, it's a very tiring job! A cable car full of people weighs 20,000 pounds. You have to use the weight of your body to pull on the lever. So actually, it is easier if you are short than if you are tall. The gripman's job is a short man's job!

Question What do you like about your job?

Al The security. It's a city job and the pay is pretty good.

Question What don't you like about it?

Al The crowds. During the tourist season, there are so many people getting on and off the car that there isn't enough room for me to pull back on the levers.

Question Has anything unusual happened on one of your runs?

Al Not really. They make a lot of movies and TV shows using the cable cars in the scenes and my shadow was in one of them!

UNIT 7 Fast Food and Takeaways

TASK 4

Most people know what a hot dog is. It's a sausage in a roll. But do you know why it's called a hot dog? Well, the long red sausage which goes into a hot dog is called a frankfurter; it got its name from the German town of Frankfurt. The sausages were very popular in the 1900s but hot frankfurters were difficult to sell in crowds. One man, Harry M Stevens, had the job of feeding the crowds in baseball games. He had an idea! Why not put the frankfurters in long, hot bread rolls? This made them easy to sell. Stevens added mustard and called them 'red-hots'.

The 'red hots' had a hot and spicy taste and became very popular. But, in 1903, an American cartoonist drew a long German sausage dog in place of the frankfurter. They were both long, and 'German', so a frankfurter in a roll soon became known as a 'hot dog'. It was a joke, but some people really thought the sausages contained dog meat! For a while, sales of hot dogs fell but not for long!

UNIT 8 Ha-ha-ha!

TASK 1

(an example of roaring laughter)

TASK 2

(examples of four different types of laughter)

TASK 6

Mrs Custard was on trial for murdering her husband. The trial took a long time and there were many problems but finally she was found guilty. The judge asked her, 'I can understand from what I've heard why you killed him. But why did you shoot him with a bow and arrow?' 'I didn't want to wake the baby,' explained Mrs Custard.

UNIT 9 Music

TASK 2

(six extracts of British folk music)

UNIT 11 Are you of age?

TASK 4

Extract 1

Interviewer What's wrong with today's teenagers?

Parent 1 That's easy – everything.

Interviewer For example?

Parent 2 They want to be treated like adults, but they won't take adult responsibilities. They just sit around, listening to loud music.

Extract 2

Interviewer Do you have any problems with your teenage children?

Parent 3 My son's fine, he works hard at school, but I have problems with my daughter Susan. She never listens to us. I think she doesn't even like us. She and her friends just use the house like a convenient hotel, and she wears these terrible clothes. I think she does it to upset us.

Extract 3

Interviewer What do you think about your parents? Paul?

Paul Well, they're so boring. I mean, they want us to be like them and accept their way of life.

Susan Yeah, they think we're all delinquents and criminals, just 'cos they don't like the way we look. They're afraid what the neighbours will think of our hair and clothes.

Paul I mean, I quite like my Mum and Dad, but they treat us like kids – always ordering us around. I think they're jealous because we have a much better time than they did when they were young.

UNIT 12 Learning to drive

TASK 6

Driving instructor Right. Is your seat belt fastened?

Student Uh huh.

Driving instructor Good. OK. Check the mirror. Is it in the right place?

Student Yes.

Driving instructor OK. Make sure the car is in neutral before you start the engine. (sound of gear stick being waggled) Right, switch on the ignition and start the car. (sound of car starting) OK, put your foot on the clutch, push it to the floor and put the car into first gear. Now look in the mirror to make sure there's nothing coming from behind. All clear?

Right, release the handbrake, lift the clutch and press the accelerator gently at the same time. Good. Go straight . . .

UNIT 16 Parents and teenagers

TASK 1

(poem of 'Little Johnny's final letter')

73

TASK 2

Extract 1

I left home at 18. My father wanted me to work and be independent so he bought me a flat and helped me to find a job in a publishing company. The job is boring and I don't earn a lot, but I have a private income, so I go abroad once or twice a year. I usually go skiing. It isn't easy but I manage.

Extract 2

I left home at 17, I suppose because I wanted to see the world. I thought it was going to be easy. You know, I'd get a well-paid job and a lovely flat. In fact, I slept on my sister's floor for six months till I got a bedsitter. I enjoy the freedom and I've got a good job in a supermarket but it is hard.

Extract 3

I left home at 16. My parents threw me out 'cos I was always in trouble. I lived with a boy for a while. Now, I'm homeless. I can't get a job because I've got nowhere to live and I can't get anywhere to live as I've got no job. Leaving home was the worst thing I ever did.

UNIT 17 Marriage

TASK 5

My parents had been looking for a boy for me for some time and a few of the ones they came up with I said no to immediately. When I met Hitesh I knew as little about him as the others my parents came up with. He seemed nicer than the others, not in a good-looking way because I don't think that's important. You see, I expected my parents with all their experience to be able to make a better choice than me.

I think arranged marriages often work out better than love marriages because you have to learn to adjust to one another. You start out with few expectations, whereas most English girls I know think it's all going to be wonderful and easy and end up disappointed.

We're very happy. I hope it lasts.

Teacher's guide

UNIT 1 A strange Island

In this unit students find out about some British habits. National and personal habits provide a source of discussion.

TASK 6

There are no 'true' answers. Encourage students to imagine what the person's life might be like.

TASK 7

Most pop magazines for young people feature profiles in which famous people talk about their lives. If you want to, use the photograph of someone who the students recognize such as a famous singer or footballer as a basis for the role play.

UNIT 2 Chips with everything

In this unit students learn something about the British diet and the way it is changing.

TASK 1

A survey on a television programme for young people showed that the favourite school food was chips.

TASK 2

Potatoes are a staple diet. In Britain people eat potato in many different forms. People are buying more and more frozen and processed potato dishes including: frozen chips; instant mash potato in powder form; crisps; and potato snacks.

TASK 3

Different countries have different staples. Base this task on a staple like rice, dumplings, pasta, etc.

The diagram shows how people in Britain are making an effort to eat more 'natural' food which contains less fat.

UNIT 3 Housing

In this unit students learn about the types of home the British live in and learn to describe different housing as well as what they expect from a home.

TASK 1

Although Britain has a very high proportion of home-owners there is still a housing problem. In the 1950s there was a programme to build multi-storey flats but these have never been popular. Today the trend is to build new estates of detached or semi-detached houses or to restore old buildings.

TASK 2

The house Andy describes is a typical semi-detached house built just after the war.

TASK 5

'Little Boxes' is a song by Pete Seeger, the American folk singer. It was written to protest about the very uniform houses in the new estates on the hillsides of San Francisco.

Little boxes on the hillside.
Little boxes made of ticky tacky,
Little boxes, little boxes,
Little boxes all the same.
There's a green one and a pink one,
And a blue one and a yellow one.
And they're all made out of ticky tacky.
And they all look just the same.

TASK 6

There are no 'correct answers' in most cases.

75

TASK 7

Unusual houses have a lot of 'character' with strange-shaped rooms, interesting surroundings, etc. However, they can be expensive to decorate, cold, isolated, etc.

UNIT 4 What is a gripman?

The San Francisco cable cars and their operators are featured in a unit about transportation and trams.

TASK 1

Further information:

The first horse tramway ran between two London suburbs, Brixton and Kennington. Shortly afterwards, tracks had been laid along most main routes, but trams were never allowed to run in to either the City or the West End.

TASK 2

It would be difficult to suggest answers here because much depends on personal taste and specific circumstances.

TASK 3

Let the students join Team A or Team B as they wish.

TASK 5

Before you listen to the interview, you may wish to teach these words:

to steer if you steer a car, boat, plane, etc, you operate it so that it goes in the direction that you want

lever a handle or bar that you pull or push in order to operate machinery

to release if you release something, you stop holding it and allow it to move or to be moved

brake a brake is a device in a vehicle that is used to make it go slower or stop

security safety from possible harm or loss

At the end of the task the student may like to plan a trip on an unusual form of transport taking in other interesting cultural or historical aspects along the way.

UNIT 5 When in Rome 1: Manners

Students consider the basis of 'good manners' and learn about what to do when they are invited to eat in Britain.

TASK 1

It is said that the British are a polite and well-mannered people. However, standards of behaviour do change, and many of the older generation think that young people today are very bad-mannered.

TASK 2

You may have to give students some local examples of good and bad manners to start them off.

TASK 4

The problems are:

a speaking with his mouth full
b reaching across for the salt
c putting her elbows on the table
d waving the knife and fork in the air
e lifting a soup bowl to his mouth

TASK 5

The order is:

soup   fish   meat   dessert   cheese

Place setting:

a soup spoon   **d** dessert spoon
b fish fork   **e** meat knife
c meat fork   **f** fish knife
                              g plate

TASK 6

RSVP – this comes from the French 'Répondez s'il vous plaît' (Please reply) and it is a polite reminder that the guest should respond to the invitation.

Here is a possible reply to the invitation:

Mr and Mrs John Brown accept with thanks your kind invitation to Dinner on Friday 6th January.

There are other possibilities, but the rule is to keep the wording very formal.

UNIT 6 When in Rome 2: Customs

Students compare ways in which people greet each other before exploring aspects of the British national character.

TASK 1

Solution:

1 kissing on the cheek	6 taking a hat off
2 saluting	7 waving
3 shaking hands	8 hugging
4 bowing	9 nodding
5 clicking the heels	10 curtsying

TASK 2

Suggested answers:

The British:

- sometimes kiss each other on one or both cheeks
- would only salute superiors
- sometimes shake hands in business contacts
- never bow except in very formal circumstances
- never click their heels
- rarely wear hats; when they do they might take it off
- might wave from a distance
- rarely hug each other except when you haven't seen someone for a while
- sometimes nod to show they accept a greeting
- only curtsy for royalty these days

TASK 3

An *understatement* is a statement which suggests that something has much less of a particular quality than it really has.

UNIT 7 Fast food and takeaways

Fast food restaurants and takeaways which serve food quickly and efficiently are a feature of life in Britain and the United States. The unit introduces students to this area and looks at some popular 'fast foods'.

TASK 1

The largest fast food chain is McDonald's. It opened in Chicago in April 1955 and in 1988 there were over 1,000 McDonald's restaurants in 46 countries. Ronald McDonald is the advertising clown for McDonald's. An amazing 96% of American school-children know who he is.

The informal atmosphere, the speed of service, the knowledge that you get the same dish in different branches, makes McDonald's very popular world-wide.

TASK 2

Although the Americans have developed modern fast food restaurants the idea is not new and many ancient cultures have fast food. A great British tradition is fish and chips.

Statements:

1 **False** The fish is usually cod or plaice, fried in batter which is a mixture of milk and flour.
2 **True**
3 **True** that traditionally fish and chips were wrapped in newspaper because newspaper retains heat. Today, however many shops feel that newspaper is not very clean and they use brown or white paper bags and wrap these up in clean paper.
4 **False** The fish is usually quite a large piece.
5 **True** Many people eat bread and butter with meals like fish and chips. Sometimes young people only buy the chips. They eat these with salt and vinegar often with their fingers.

TASK 4

On the tape is the true story of the 'hot dog'.

TASK 5

Answers:

1 True
2 False Stevens called them 'red-hots'.
3 False Stevens wanted a way of selling sausages, quickly and easily.
4 False The word became popular after the cartoon in 1903.
5 False Hot dogs do not always contain mustard today.

TASK 6

The aim of the task is to carry out a survey on hamburger-eating. Avoid this task if many of your students do not eat hamburgers.

TASK 7

As the section suggests convenience foods are very popular in Britain and for many people the snacks replace regular meals. Although the products have different names and tastes they are, in fact, very similar and the names, shapes, etc. are chosen for particular age groups.

UNIT 8 Ha-ha-ha!

The aim of this unit is to look at humour. Paradoxically, humour is one of the most serious subjects. Or as Frigyes Karinthy, a 20th century Hungarian writer put it, 'I can stand no kidding in humour'.

TASK 1

Sebastien Chamfort was a French writer from the 18th century.

On the tape is an example of roaring laughter.

TASK 2

Dr Samuel Johnson was an 18th century English thinker.

On the cassette is an example of four types of laughter. They could best be described as:

1 restrained
2 hearty
3 polite
4 unnatural
(These are only suggestions.)

TASK 3

The zoo in San Diego is considered to be one of the richest animal parks in the US.

TASK 4

Script-writing should be assigned as homework.

TASK 5

Punch is a weekly humorous and satirical magazine, founded in 1841. It has a circulation of nearly 90,000.

TASK 6

Listen to the joke.
Since there is no time in class to prepare a joke it would be best done as a homework task.

UNIT 9 Music

In this unit students:
- *learn to talk about different forms of music including folk and choral music,*
- *discuss the risks from loud music.*

TASK 2

On the cassette are six extracts of folk music from the British Isles.

Extract	Comes from
1	Scotland
2	Wales
3	England
4	Ireland
5	Ireland
6	England

TASK 3

There are no 'right' or 'wrong' answers. Encourage students to discuss their choices.

TASK 6

Initially, the *Walkman* was a trademark for the Sony Corporation of Japan. Today, the term is used for all the small portable cassette recorders with headphones that are also known as personal stereos. In England and America many people use Walkmans while on their way to and from school, work, etc. Apart from the dangers to hearing there are other problems. For example, a young English girl who was listening to a Walkman, was murdered by an attacker she did not hear. Apart from the Walkman, young people also carry large cassette recorders around. These are known as 'ghetto blasters' and they play very loud music.

UNIT 10 A question of sport

In this unit students:

- *learn the names of the most popular indoor and outdoor sports in Britain and talk about popular games at home,*
- *talk about competitive sport and team games,*
- *explore football hooliganism,*
- *explore sexism in sport.*

TASK 1

The sports are:

1 **Fishing**—one of the most popular individual sports (note that most of the fish are put back in the river or lake!).
2 **Football**—a game the English claim to have invented.
3 **Tennis**—the annual championship at the All England Tennis Club in Wimbledon, South London is still the greatest tournament in the world.
4 **Rugby**—a game in which fifteen players try to carry an oval ball across the line of the opposition.
5 **Squash**—indoor game played in an enclosed court. The ball is a small rubber ball and the racket is like a tennis racket but smaller and lighter. The ball is hit off any wall but must hit the front wall above a line painted above the floor. Outside Britain squash is popular in Australia, New Zealand and for years the world champion has been from Pakistan.
6 **Darts**—an indoor game that is very popular in pubs and clubs. The steel darts are thrown at a circular board (the dart board). The aim is to score points which are subtracted from the original total of 301 or 501.
7 **Snooker**—a game like billiards played with fifteen red balls and six coloured balls (yellow, green, brown, blue, pink and black) and a white cue ball. Players use cues to try to remove all the balls from the table in a certain order. Snooker is one of the most popular television sports in Britain.
8 **Golf**—invented in Scotland it is now played all over the world.
9 **Cricket**—the English national game which is also played with great enthusiasm in countries which were colonies like the West Indies, Pakistan, Australia, New Zealand.
10 **Cycling**—in parts of England, especially Oxford and Cambridge, the cycle is used as a means of transport as well as a source of exercise.
11 **Bowls**—a game where players try to put a heavy wooden ball as close to a small white ball or jack as possible. It is played on very smooth lawns or on carpets indoors.
12 **Badminton**—an indoor rackets game played with a feather shuttlecock rather than a ball.

American sports:

a American football   c baseball
b basketball   d ten-pin bowling

American football is the fastest growing team game in Britain.

TASK 4

There is no real agreement as to the cause of the 'English disease'. People blame the social conditions, alcohol, the fact there is no military service in Britain, etc. There is however some evidence that 'hooligans' are in fact very well-organized gangs who like to fight and cause damage. Members come from every class of society but what makes people do this?

TASK 5

Women in Britain are now more equal in sport than they used to be. For example, female tennis players earn almost as much as the men but there is still very little football played by women. This is very different from countries like Italy where there are women professionals. Some events like Henley (the Wimbledon of rowing) are still 'men-only'.

UNIT 11 Are you of age?

In this unit students explore some of the legal rights of young people and see how disagreement over what young people can and cannot do is a source of conflict and intolerance.

TASK 1

The illustrations show twenty-first and 'coming of age' cards. Traditionally, young people get a key to the house when they come of age.

TASK 4

UNIT 12 Learning to drive

This unit aims to get students talking and thinking about the steps we go through in learning to drive by comparing the system in their country with the British one.

TASK 4

The Highway Code is a book of rules for road users. It contains information about road signs, crossing the road, driving on motorways, etc. Everyone learning to drive has to be familiar with the signs in the Highway Code.

Solution:

1 H 2 B 3 G 4 E 5 C 6 A 7 D 8 F

80

TASK 6

UNIT 13 Cruelty to animals

Britain is justifiably known as a nation of animal lovers and recently there has been a lot of controversy about the way that animals are being treated. Students learn about the main issues and some of the many animal welfare organizations in Britain.

TASK 1

H G Wells was a well known science fiction novelist in the early 20th century. He is perhaps best known for his *War of the Worlds*. The synopsis is an introduction to the photographs which explore:

- cruelty to animals through activities like *battery farming* where farmers aim to produce a maximum number of eggs, etc. by keeping animals in small places.
- cruelty (?) in training animals to perform.
- cruelty (?) in treating animals like humans.

TASK 2

As the text indicates there are over 380 UK charities and societies which aim to protect animals. Some of them have an international impact and issues such as the treatment of animals in traditional celebrations as well as the eating of dogs and cats, regularly feature in the popular British press. This task introduces students to some of the groups and what they do.

TASK 4

Vivisection is a very emotive issue in the UK. Your students may wish to find out more about vivisection in their country.

TASK 5

An opportunity for any animal loving students to do a mini project.

UNIT 14 Charity industry

This unit discusses many different ways of raising money for charity.

TASK 1

Save the Children fund helps the starving children in the world.

Oxfam sends aid to third world countries to help the starving and those made homeless through natural disasters like earthquakes or flooding.

The **RSPCA** works to prevent any cruel treatment being done to animals.

The **British Heart Foundation** collects money for research into the prevention and treatment of heart disease.

UNIT 15 At a guess

The main idea throughout this unit is that people are often misled by all kinds of stereotypes.

TASK 1

The people shown in the photographs *really* pursue the occupations indicated. We seek to prove with this task and the next one how easily one can be tricked by appearances.

Solution:

1 architect	4 removal man
2 street cleaner	5 farmer
3 editor	6 university student

TASK 3

Other crude generalizations about the British are:

British food is awful.
Brits always make compromises.
They foster a spirit of fair play.
English people are cold and reserved.
Scottish people are stingy.
The Irish drink a lot of alcohol.
Every Welshman sings beautifully.

TASK 4

Solution:

1 Paul Newman	4 Humphrey Bogart
2 John Travolta	5 Robert Redford
3 Sylvester Stallone	6 Henry Fonda

Films featuring the actors in the photos:

Paul Newman: *Butch Cassidy and the Sundance Kid, Cat on a Hot Tin Roof, The Sting*
John Travolta: *Grease, Saturday Night Fever, Staying Alive*
Sylvester Stallone: *Rocky, F.I.S.T., Rambo*
Humphrey Bogart: *Casablanca, Swing Your Lady, The Love Lottery*
Robert Redford: *War Hunt, The Great Waldo Pepper, All the President's Men*
Henry Fonda: *Young Mr Lincoln, Main Street to Broadway, On Golden Pond*
Yul Brynner, Peter Falk, Dustin Hoffman or **Charles Bronson** are certainly not very good-looking 'good guys'.

TASK 5

Suggested answers:

thin lips malicious	**blue eyes** naïve
long fingers artistic	**pointed nose** curious

UNIT 16   Parents and teenagers

This unit looks at the relationship between parents and teenagers as a background to leaving home.

TASK 1

The poem on page 63 is on tape.

Most young people eventually leave home. However, a small number just run away. Sometimes, parents do not know where their children are and unless they are under sixteen the police do not force them to return when they find them. There are groups that encourage children to telephone or write home so that their parents know they are alive. Brian Patten's poem is such a 'letter' and raises issues such as:

■ the panic parents feel when their children disappear;

- the reasons why children run away such as wanting to be adult and the 'excitement' of the city (*lines 11–16*);
- the loneliness all round (*lines 18–21*).

TASK 2

Possible answers:

	Extract 1	Extract 2	Extract 3
When	18	17	16
Why	father wanted her to work, be independent	wanted to see world and work	thrown out for mis-behaving
Job	publishing company	supermarket	unemployed
Lives	own flat	bedsitter	homeless

People who are 'homeless' may live with 'friends', in special temporary 'hostels' or even in the streets.

TASK 3

In New South Wales, Australia, youngsters can go to the courts if they have problems with their parents.

UNIT 17 Marriage

This unit is about marriage. By giving information about marriage in Britain it encourages discussion about:

- *when and where people get married;*
- *how they get married (the nature of the ceremony) and the vows (or promises) they make;*
- *marital traditions in the students' own countries;*
- *mixed marriages (between people of different races or religion);*
- *arranged marriages (where it is the parents who decide on the partners).*

TASK 1

Divorce in Britain is still a relatively complicated process and couples must live separately until the divorce is final. In some cases, the male partner has to pay to support his ex-wife and children after the divorce. Despite this, divorce is increasing.

TASK 2

an engagement – an arrangement two people make to get married

banns – public announcement that two people are going to marry. The vicar reads out the banns in church

the best man – his job is to help the bridegroom. He is usually a very close friend.

bridesmaids – women/girls who help the bride with her flowers, etc. Bridesmaids are usually close friends or members of the family.

page boy – young boy who helps with the dress and the train (the long back part of her dress).

'something old, something new' etc. – Brides may borrow old shoes, a friend's jewellery, wear a blue ribbon, etc.

vows – the promises a couple make to each other during the marriage ceremony.

thee – you

holy ordinance – law

and thereto I plight thee my troth – I make this promise to you

Notice the importance given to marriage as something permanent until the partner dies (till death do us part);

Notice also the woman promises to obey her husband. In the modern version a woman can choose not to say this.

confetti – small pieces of coloured paper that people throw over the bride and groom.

honeymoon – holiday taken by a man and woman who have just got married.

TASK 3

A mini project. Students can complete an album or a simple wall display. Make sure students display their work or exchange albums.

TASK 5

As the listening implies, the system has advantages and disadvantages. For young people in the Indian and Pakistani community in Britain (sometimes referred to as the Asians) arranged marriages are a problem because:

- they prevent integration;
- they make Asians 'different';
- they stop young Asians from going out freely with members of the opposite sex in an open society.